Culturally Competent Practice

A Series from
Children's Voice Magazine

CWLA Press • Washington, DC

CWLA Press is an imprint of the Child Welfare League of America.

The Child Welfare League of America (CWLA) is a North American, privately supported, nonprofit, membership-based organization committed to preserving, protecting, and promoting the well-being of all children and their families. Believing that children are our most valuable resource, CWLA, through its membership, advocates for high standards, sound public policies, and quality services for children and their families in need.

Understanding Asian Family Values © 1996 Walter Philips

Supporting African American Familes © 1997 Family Resource Coalition

Programs with a Cultural Fit © 1997 Elba Montalvo

The World View of American Indian Families © 1995 School of Human Ecology, University of Wisconsin–Madison

All rights reserved. Neither this book nor any part may be reproduced or transmitted in any form or by any means, electronic or mechanical, including photocopying, microfilming, and recording, or by any information storage and retrieval system, without permission in writing from the publisher. For information on this or other CWLA publications, contact the CWLA Publications Department at the address below.

CHILD WELFARE LEAGUE OF AMERICA, INC.
440 First Street NW, Third Floor, Washington, DC 20001-2085
E-mail: books@cwla.org

CURRENT PRINTING (last digit)
10 9 8 7 6 5 4 3 2 1

Cover design by Jennifer R. Geanakos
Text design by Steve Boehm

Printed in the United States of America
ISBN # 0–87868–704-1

Contents

Introduction ... *v*

Understanding Asian Family Values ... *1*
    Walter Philips

Supporting African American Families:
    Dispelling Myths, Building on Strengths ... *7*
    Robert B. Hill

Programs with a Cultural Fit:
    Working with Latino Families ... *15*
    Elba Montalvo

The World View of American Indian Families ... *23*
    Terry L. Cross

Introduction

Cultural competence is the ability to provide services effectively to people of all cultures, races, ethnic backgrounds, and religions in a way that recognizes, values, affirms, and respects the worth of individuals and protects and preserves their dignity. But to respond respectfully and effectively to people of different cultural backgrounds, service providers must first understand the widely differing cultures of the people they serve.

The articles in this monograph were published as a four-part series in *Children's Voice*. The articles, all of which originally appeared elsewhere, are individually copyrighted by their respective authors as indicated herein and are reprinted here by permission.

Understanding Asian Family Values

*by Walter Philips**

Asian Americans are one of the fastest growing cultural groups in the United States. The Asian population is diverse, covering a range of ethnicities, cultures, and languages. Asian Americans vary in terms of immigration and refugee experiences, acculturation levels, and socioeconomic levels.

Despite this great diversity, practitioners working with children and families should be aware of some of the common values among Asian Americans and take them into consideration when working with Asian families. These values stem from principles in three main Eastern philosophies: Buddhism, Confucianism, and Taoism.

BUDDHISM

Buddhism provides a spiritual structure for many Asians. Buddhists view time as circular rather than linear. Many Asians believe in the concepts of reincarnation and karma. Simply stated, karma refers to the notion that what happens to you in this life is due to your behaviors and actions in your past life, and your behaviors and actions in this life will dictate what will happen to you in the next.

Because of this belief, many Asians will endure their pain and suffering in this life in acceptance of their fate. Often, this may leave a

---

* Walter Philips is the manager of behavioral health, Union of Pan Asian Communities, San Diego, California. Published in the Winter 1997 issue of *Children's Voice,* this article was adapted from Volume 10, Number 1, 1996, of *The Roundtable,* the journal of the National Resource Center for Special Needs Adoption, Spaulding for Children, Southfield, Michigan. © 1996 Walter Philips person little motivation to change. Successfully using the concept that one's actions impact one's next life may help practitioners to create motivation for change in someone who previously had none.

Confucianism

A major principle of Confucianism is filial piety. This notion defines specific rules of conduct in social relationships and places great importance on the family. Several key concepts follow from the principle of filial piety:

- Family roles are highly structured, hierarchical, male-dominated, and paternally oriented.

- The welfare and integrity of the family are of great importance. The individual is expected to submerge or repress emotions, desires, behaviors, and individual goals to further the family welfare and to maintain its reputation. The individual is obligated to save face so as to not bring shame onto the family. The incentive, therefore, is to keep problems within the family.

- Interdependency is valued and stems from the strong sense of obligation to the family. This concept influences relationships among family members. The family provides support and assistance for each individual member; in turn, individual members provide support and assistance for the entire family. These relationships, interactions, and obligations are lifelong; and the goal of individual members is not necessarily autonomy and independence. This concept is critical to understanding Asian families, and service providers should avoid applying Western labels such as "codependency" and "enmeshment" when observing normal family functioning dictated by cultural values and beliefs.

TAOISM

Taoism defines one's relationship with nature. According to this philosophy, maintaining harmony and balance with nature is important to one's spiritual well-being. The goal of many of the traditional healing practices, such as herbal medicine, acupuncture, coining, and cupping, is to restore this delicate balance. In Asian families, this concept extends to maintaining harmony in social relationships. Because of this, practitioners may observe that:

- Families and individual family members may seek to avoid conflict and confrontation with others.

- An individual may appear passive, indifferent, or indecisive. The person may fear that taking the initiative could lead to disagreement or conflict.

- The individual may be overtly compliant and agreeable when, in fact, he or she disagrees with the other person.

RESPONDING WITH CULTURAL COMPETENCE

These principles supply a framework for understanding many of the Asian families with whom child welfare practitioners may work. Remember that these are generalizations; not all Asian Americans hold these values, and most Asians do not consciously follow these principles. Rather, they have become ingrained in broader family values and practices that have formed over centuries.

Service providers should integrate these concepts into their work with Asian Americans. The following suggestions will help child welfare practitioners begin providing culturally competent services for Asian American families.

- When assessing Asian American families, practitioners should gather information regarding specific families' ethnic backgrounds, languages, immigration and refugee experiences, acculturation levels, and community support systems.

- Develop trust by establishing and adhering to rules of social conduct and proper social interaction.

- Attempt to maintain and, if appropriate, reestablish traditional family structures according to cultural norms. Respect the family hierarchy.

- Use extended family members for support systems; lines between nuclear families and extended families are not as rigid in Asian families as they are in Western culture.

- Allow families and their individual members opportunities to save face whenever possible.

- Avoid creating situations that may lead to conflict and confrontation. Rather, use indirect methods of communication, when appropriate, to make a point.

- Because Asians prefer to keep problems within the family, maintaining confidentiality is critical. Families must be assured that their problems will not become public knowledge.

- Service providers must be active and offer tangible interventions for Asian Americans. Passivity in the worker may be viewed as lack of expertise and authority. Many Asian American families are seeking concrete, tangible solutions to their problems and are uncomfortable with process- and insight-oriented strategies.

This article cannot provide all the knowledge and skills necessary to be culturally competent with Asian Americans. Hopefully, however, it will supply some beginning strategies in working with Asian American families and children. Remember that Asian Americans comprise a diverse group of people who should be assessed individually when developing appropriate intervention strategies. Cultural competence starts with sensitivity and appreciation for diversity and integrates acquired knowledge of cultures with practice skills and techniques. Begin integrating some of these concepts regarding Asian values into your service delivery.

Supporting African American Families

Dispelling Myths, Building on Strengths

*by Robert B. Hill**

Many observers wrongly believe that the problems of inner-city families are intractable. The news media devote considerable space documenting the crisis with negative statistics about African American families. By blaming the victims—attributing the crisis to internal deficits or weaknesses such as female-headed families, poor work ethics, and underclass values, rather than to such external constraints as racism, recessions, inflation, the exodus of industries from inner cities, and anti-poor public policies—they focus on identifying problems and not on generating solutions.

African American families have many assets: strong achievement aspirations, strong work orientations, flexible family roles, strong kinship bonds, and strong religious orientations. Although these attributes characterize many racial and ethnic groups, they have manifested themselves differently in African American families because of their unique history. Family support practitioners can work more effectively with families of color by building on these strengths.

---

*   Robert B. Hill, Ph.D., is the director of the Institute for Urban Research, Morgan State University, Baltimore, Maryland. This article, published in the Spring 1997 issue of *Children's Voice*, was adapted from the Spring 1993 issue of *Family Resource Coalition Report*. © 1997 Family Resource Coalition.

High Aspirations

Research has found that, although they score lower than Caucasian children on standardized tests, African American children often have higher educational and occupational aspirations than Caucasian children of similar economic status. Puzzled by these findings, some social scientists have explained this result in terms of pathology. Characterizing these lofty goals as too high and unrealistic, they concluded that educators should lower aspirations to prevent African American children from becoming frustrated as adults.

Unfortunately, many studies have revealed that bright inner-city children in the public schools encounter "misguidance" counselors who lower their aspirations and self-esteem to such an extent that they drop out in record numbers. Inner-city children need educators who can help them attain their high aspirations.

One of the most successful educational initiatives that reinforce the high-achievement orientation of inner-city children and their parents is Head Start. This preschool program emphasizes parental participation and has encouraged higher achievement among thousands of low-income children.

Another effective program for African American youth is College Here We Come, which seeks to raise the educational and occupational horizons of young people in public housing. Launched in 1974 by residents of a public housing complex in Washington, D.C., this initiative has provided social and economic support helping more than 600 low-income youth attend college.

Also in Washington, PROJECT 2000 is an early-intervention program that enhances the academic performance of African American boys, especially those from single-parent, female-headed households. African American educator Spencer Holland created this program in collaboration with Concerned Black Men to counteract the so-called fourth-grade syndrome—the alienation of African American boys from school as they reach the fourth grade. Holland asks adult men to volunteer as assistants in Grades 1 through 3 to provide positive male role models in the primary grades. The program has expanded to three elementary schools in Baltimore, Maryland. An analysis of the program's pilot year reveals it has had immediate positive effects.

Simba ("young lion" in Swahili) is a comprehensive male-socialization program that prepares African American boys ages 7 through 19 for responsible manhood. Begun in Chicago, Simba presents positive adult male roles, develops life skills, enhances ethnic and cultural identity, raises self-esteem and academic performance, and promotes healthy male-female relationships. Similar rites-of-passage programs for girls and boys have been developed throughout the country.

STRONG WORK ETHIC

Despite popular belief that most African Americans are on welfare, U.S. census data reveal that only about one-fifth of all African American families—and only half of low-income African American families—received public assistance in the 1980s.

Even so, African American groups have developed numerous innovative programs to reduce welfare dependency. Some of the most effective come from resident management corporations of public housing. These groups maintain safe, pleasant, comfortable living environments more efficiently and cost-effectively than can local housing authorities. As a result of tenant management, vandalism, welfare dependency, school dropout, teenage pregnancy, and unemployment have declined sharply, while building repairs and rent collections have risen, indicating an increase in neighborhood stability.

One key to the success of public housing is the hiring of former welfare recipients to operate local small businesses. Maintenance, day care, laundry, tailoring, barbering, beauty care, catering, reverse commuting, and thrift shop initiatives abound throughout the nation.

Several innovative programs are advancing entrepreneurship among inner-city youth, attempting to apply young drug dealers' superb self-employment skills to legal activities. For example, the Educational Training and Enterprise Center in Camden, New Jersey, has helped hundreds of youth create businesses in food vending, maintenance, security, and sales. A former police officer has developed a mini-mall at Woodson Junior High School in Washington, D.C., comprising about 10 student-operated small businesses.

FLEXIBLE FAMILY ROLES

In African American families, mothers and fathers often assume some of the traditional roles of the other, and children perform some parental functions for younger siblings. This role adaptability has contributed to the stability and advancement of two-parent African American households.

Role flexibility is most evident in the disproportionate number of African American families headed by women. Traditionally, single-parent families headed by women are depicted as broken or pathological, whereas two-parent families are described as intact or healthy. But such characterizations mistake family structure for family functioning. One-parent families are often more intact or cohesive than two-parent families: Data show higher rates of child abuse, domestic violence, and runaway children among suburban, two-parent families than among single-parent families in inner cities.[†]

Programs targeted at young, single, African American mothers, designed to strengthen single-parent families, abound in inner-city communities nationwide. One such effort is the Sisterhood of Black Single Mothers in Bedford-Stuyvesant, Brooklyn, New York. This program has shown that circumstances of low-income single mothers can be improved markedly by addressing their needs from a holistic perspective; by enhancing their sense of self-worth; and by developing their skills in parenting, male-female relationships, education, and employment. The program, which started by helping

---

[†] R. Hill. (1981). *Economic Policies and Black Progress.* Washington, DC: National Urban League.

single mothers to complete their high-school equivalency, has motivated many to graduate from college.

Numerous communities have developed programs to enhance the parenting skills of African American fathers. One of the earliest, launched by the National Urban League, is targeted at adolescent and young African American males. The program promotes responsible sexuality, seeks to prevent out-of-wedlock pregnancies, and teaches participants to assume appropriate parental responsibility for their children. Implemented by the Urban League affiliates across the country, these programs provide a range of educational, training, and support services.

KINSHIP BONDS

According to conventional wisdom, the extended family has declined sharply in urban areas. Research reveals, however, that the proportion of African American extended families has increased. U.S. census data reveal that, between 1970 and 1980, African American extended-family households rose from 23% to 28%. By 1992, according to the University of Wisconsin's National Survey of Households, two out of five African American households were three-generational. Further, African American extended families often reach beyond individual households and may include members who are not related by blood or marriage.

Social welfare policies and family support programs must make better use of kinship networks. Policymakers and child welfare systems must recognize the range of services that kinship networks provide in such areas as day care, support to unwed mothers, informal adoption, and foster care.

Kinship networks often provide short-term child care, especially for working parents. About two-fifths of working African Americans depend on responsible relatives for day care. Kinship networks also provide support to unwed mothers. Nine out of 10 babies born to African American teenagers live in three-generational households.

Studies have found that adolescent mothers who have the support of kin are more likely to avoid welfare dependency, and their children's development is healthier, than teenage mothers who raise their children without assistance from relatives.‡

Informal adoption has been a major support in African American families since antiquity, with children living with grandparents or aunts and uncles for varying lengths of time. During slavery, thousands of African American children were reared by their grandmothers. According to U.S. census data, the number of African American children living with relatives has risen from 1.3 million (13%) in 1970 to 1.6 million (16%) in 1990.

Even though African American families provide extensive informal adoption and foster care services, many child welfare systems have not targeted kinship networks for such services until recently. Of the one million African American children who live in households without either parent present, 80% are informally adopted by kin; the remaining 20% are in foster care. While the government could not find permanent homes for these 200,000 foster children, the African American kinship network succeeded in finding homes for 800,000 children. Yet, because children of color still account for most children in foster care, there is an urgent need for public policies that encourage relatives to take in children and motivate systems to use kinship networks as major placement resources.

Many community groups provide innovative adoption and family preservation services that reinforce kinship networks. One of the oldest, Homes for Black Children (HBC), was founded in Detroit in the late 1960s. Alarmed by the large number of African American children available for adoption but languishing in foster care, HBC has demonstrated there are more than enough African American families willing to provide wholesome environments for children who need homes. From 1984 to 1993, HBC found adoptive homes for more than 700 African American children. HBC now places greater

---

‡   F. Furstenburg Jr., J. Brooks-Gunn, and S. Philip Morgan. (1987). *Adolescent Mothers in Later Life.* Cambridge, England: Cambridge University Press.

emphasis on family preservation to prevent unnecessary foster care placements.

Religious Orientation

Religion plays a strong role in the lives of African Americans. In a 1981 Gallup poll, 67% of African Americans said that religion was "very important" in their lives. A 1980 National Urban League survey found that 76% of African Americans belong to churches and 67% attend church at least monthly.

As the most dominant institution in the African American community, churches provide a range of social services to strengthen families and enhance child development. Turning to holistic approaches to meet the needs of inner-city families, African American churches are establishing Quality of Life Centers, whose services include day care, preschool programs, nurseries, parenting education, family counseling, remedial education, family planning, substance abuse prevention, employment training, recreational activities, and youth programs.

Historically, African American churches have assisted orphans and homeless children. Most of the early African American orphanages were founded by African American religious institutions. Recently, the disproportionate number of African American children in foster care has alarmed many ministers. In 1980, Father George Clement of Chicago founded One Church, One Child, in which African American churches commit to adopting at least one foster child. This program has been replicated by churches nationwide.

African Americans with strong religious orientations achieve higher socioeconomic levels than those with little religious commitment. A 1980 study of young males in low-income communities, conducted by the National Bureau of Economic Research, concluded that a deep religious commitment was strongly correlated with lower rates of school dropout, delinquency, out-of-wedlock births, and drug abuse.

Clearly, African American families have many unique and powerful assets. By dispelling myths about African American families and building instead on their strengths, family support practitioners have at their disposal major resources to help support inner-city families.

Programs with a Cultural Fit

Working with Latino Families

by Elba Montalvo*

One of the major problems in foster care and adoption today is the lack of cultural competence in services to Latino children. Inconceivably, creating cultural bridges to meet the needs of the large numbers of African American and Latino children in foster care is still not common practice in human services.

The Council on Adoptable Children developed the first Hispanic Adoption Program in 1978 in New York. At that time, Latino children, who accounted for one-fourth of the city's foster care population, were systematically placed along color lines in foster care and adoptive homes. Dark-skinned Latino children were placed with African American families, lighter-skinned children with Caucasian families. To stop that practice, a group of Latino professionals in 1982 founded the Committee for Hispanic Children and Families (CHCF), a nonprofit, community-based organization advocating for Latino families.

Implemented in 1979, the Child Welfare Reform Act (CWRA) emphasized prevention over foster care and keeping kids in their communities. CWRA stressed permanency planning—securing permanent homes for children rather than warehousing them in foster

---

* Elba Montalvo is the executive director of the Committee for Hispanic Children and Families, New York, New York; chair of the Council of Latino Executives in Child Welfare; and a member of CWLA's Board of Directors. This article was published in the Summer 1997 issue of *Children's Voice* and was adapted from Vol. 8, No. 2, 1994, of *The Roundtable,* the journal of the National Resource Center for Special Needs Adoption, Spaulding for Children, Southfield, Michigan. © 1997 Elba Montalvo.

care. The idea of placing kids with relatives, however—kinship care—was not common practice; the prevailing assumption was that extended family members were unsuitable caregivers. If African American and Latino professionals had been involved in policymaking, kinship care would have likely been part of CWRA. Despite this, CWRA did improve the foster care system. Children were moved toward permanency more quickly—either returned to parents or moved toward adoption. It also stopped the automatic placement of children in institutions.

Unfortunately, however, services have not changed dramatically for Latino children. Generally, agencies serving Latino children continue to invalidate their culture by omission. Latinos do not feel welcomed by these agencies because nothing about the agencies reflect Latino culture—not the people who work there, nor office decorations. Their services are not designed with the Latino population in mind.

THE LATINO POPULATION

Many people do not know there are 21 Spanish-speaking countries—and Brazil is not one of them. Although Latinos speak the same language and share similar values and a heritage from Spain, there are vast differences among national groups. Latinos are not monolithic, and treating all Latinos alike is a mistake. Family-serving agencies must understand the particular characteristics of Latino groups in their areas—such as immigration status; history; religious background (not all are Catholics); ethnic makeup (the mix of indigenous populations and African and European ancestry); and reasons for migration.

According to the U.S. Census Bureau, more than 23 million Latinos, including four million families, live in the United States. Latinos make up 9% of the nation's population. Spoken by 17.3 million people, Spanish is the second most common language in American homes. Between 1980 and 1990, the U.S. Latino population increased by 53%, seven times the rate of the non-Latino population. By the year 2000, Latinos will outnumber African Americans, constituting the largest minority group in the United States.

Mexicans are the largest Latino group, numbering nearly 13.5 million people. Puerto Ricans are the second largest group, with over 2.7 million people. Cubans make up the third largest group, with slightly over 1 million. Nearly 90% of Latinos live in just 10 states: Arizona, California, Colorado, Florida, Illinois, Massachusetts, New Jersey, New Mexico, New York, and Texas. California is home to more than one-third of the Latino population.

Understanding Differences

There is no secret formula for working with Latino families with cultural competence. It takes hard work, commitment, and resources. It takes programs with a cultural fit. When programs are culturally ignorant, prospective adoptive families will leave, and children will either be placed in non-Latino homes or linger in the foster care system. To provide quality services to Latino families, including children placed in adoptive homes, we need to strive for cultural competence.

The first step is self-awareness and acceptance of differences. We must be conscious of mainstream American values, because they affect us on a personal level and are reflected in the attitudes and policies of child welfare agencies. The cultural aspects to consider include such concepts as nonverbal communication, body motion, and use of space. We are not always aware of them, yet they prevent communication with and proper assessment and treatment of clients whose cultures are different from our own. For example, if I were to pucker my lips and look in a certain direction, that is Puerto Rican nonverbal communication for "look at that or at that one." One can have a whole conversation in Puerto Rican without speaking a word.

Latino families can be lost through trivial misunderstandings. For example, ignoring a prospective adoptive Latino couple while they are sitting in a waiting room could cause them to feel rejected and lead to alienation. Latino families considering adoption need an opportunity to know their adoption specialists and place them within a familial context before proceeding with the business at hand.

Other values shared by most Latino national groups include the importance of the extended family, the interdependence of family members, differentiation of gender roles, unconditional respect for adults, and deference to authority.† In mainstream American culture, on the other hand, respect is earned, not based on status.

Latino culture also differs from Anglo culture in its concept of time and time orientation. Latino culture tends to be polychronic and oriented to the present. To understand what polychronic means, consider an extended Latino family gathering, in which numerous interactions and conversations are taking place, often overlapping one another. A North American family, particularly with Anglo roots, might view the multiple simultaneous interactions as confusing and noisy. Anglo culture stresses talking one at a time; interrupting is impolite. In a Latino family, the stress is on the involvement of people and the completion of transactions rather than on adherence to preset schedules. In a present orientation, what is happening at this moment is what is important; only God can control what will happen tomorrow.

In contrast, mainstream American values have a monochronic time orientation, emphasizing schedules, segmentation, and promptness. Not that Latinos don't recognize the importance of being on time, but especially in social situations, "on time" is much more fluid for Latinos. Anglo culture is also heavily oriented to the future, planning for tomorrow. On the opposite end of the spectrum, Asian cultures are often oriented to the past, emphasizing the importance of ancestry, family history, and traditions.

---

† N. Garcia-Preto. (1996). "Puerto Rican Families." In M. McGoldrick, J. Giordano, & J.K. Pearce (Eds.), *Ethnicity and Family Therapy.* (pp. 169–171). New York: Guilford Press.

TRANSCULTURAL ADOPTIONS

Latino children are still placed in non-Latino homes where their cultural background is ignored. They grow up believing there is something wrong with their heritage or that it is unimportant because their adoptive parents do not recognize, acknowledge, or celebrate their children's Latino background.

Children are best served when placed in homes that give them continuity. Homes that are culturally similar to the homes of their biological parents can provide a continuity of care that is critical for children's healthy development. For optimal continuity of care, a relative's home is the best alternative. If a relative's home is unavailable or inappropriate, the next best home is that of someone from the child's own culture. For Latinos, this means a home of the same national group—Puerto Rican children in Puerto Rican homes, for example, or Cuban children in Cuban homes. If a home of the same national group is not available, then another Latino home is best.

Only if no Latino home is available should a non-Latino home be considered—and then it should be a home that values and is knowledgeable about the child's Latino culture. When evaluating whether a non-Latino home is appropriate for placing a Latino child, agencies should consider such questions as whether the family has Latino friends who can serve as role models for the child and whether the family lives in or has access to a Latino community. CHCF agrees with other child advocates that providing children the opportunity to live in loving, permanent homes of any race or cultural background is preferable to their growing up without permanent homes.

RECRUITING LATINO FAMILIES

Terry Cross, executive director of the National Indian Child Welfare Association, defines individual cultural competence as "the state of being capable of functioning effectively in the context of cultural differences". For the organization, he defines cultural competence as "a set of congruent practice skills, attitudes, policies, and structures, which come together in a system, agency, or among professionals and enable that system, agency, or those professionals to work effectively in the context of cultural differences."‡

In adoption agencies, cultural competence includes the successful recruitment of families of color. Whatever venue agencies choose to recruit Latino families, materials should be conceived and written first in Spanish, then translated to English. Because of differences in communication styles among national groups, agencies must also keep in mind the particular Latino populations with whom they are working. Some Latinos are more formal than others in language and expressive behaviors. For example, South Americans are more formal than Latinos from the Caribbean; and there are also language and regional differences.

Additionally, although Spanish is the second most common language in 39 states and the District of Columbia, only 8 states require bilingual investigations. Most states often use children as translators—a practice that can negatively impact family roles.

The question is whether agencies are making genuine efforts to embrace people who only speak the Spanish language.

BIENVENIDOS LATINOS

Agencies and social workers who provide services to Latino children and families should consider several issues:

- Build the necessary bridges. Latinos are not asking adoption specialists to change their own values but rather to understand the values of Latinos and to incorporate them into their practices.

---

‡ People of Color Leadership Institute and National Indian Child Welfare Association. (1993). *Training Guidebook for Developing Cultural Competence*. Washington, DC: People of Color Leadership Institute and Portland, OR: National Indian Child Welfare Association.

- On an organizational level, cultural competence requires agencies to adopt policies and programs, from the reception area to program design, that say, "Bienvenidos Latinos"—Welcome Latinos.
- Bilingual personnel are critical.
- Collecting data to reflect ethnic breakdown in all categories, programs, and services enables providers to better understand the needs of Latino children and assists in designing programs with a cultural fit.

To create quality programs for Latino children and make services Latino friendly will take all of us—adoptive parents, social workers, policymakers, administrators, and legislators; Latinos, African Americans, Caucasians, Asian Americans, and Native Americans. It takes all of us to care about each other's children.

The World View of American Indian Families

by Terry L. Cross*

World view is the collective thought process of a people or cultural group. Thoughts generate into ideas. Ideas collect and become concepts. Concepts come together to become constructs. Constructs become paradigms. Paradigms link to create a world view. By the time we get to world view, however, it is pretty hard to describe.

One cannot describe something as broad as a world view without overgeneralizing and oversimplifying. For the sake of discussion, however, such oversimplification allows us to examine differences between world views. Two world views are dominant today—linear and relational. Family resilience among native peoples and many other people of color can be understood from the relational view.

THE LINEAR VIEW

In this country, however, the mainstream world view is linear. The linear world view is rooted in European and mainstream American thought. It is temporal and firmly rooted in the logic of cause and effect.

---

* Terry Cross is a member of the Seneca Nation of Indians and is the executive director of the National Indian Child Welfare Association, Portland, Oregon. This article, published in the Fall 1997 issue of *Children's Voice,* is based on the author's keynote address at the conference, Resiliency in Families: Racial and Ethnic Minority Families in America, University of Wisconsin-Madison, May 31–June 2, 1994, which was published in *Ethnic Minority Families: Native and Immigrant American Families (Vol. 1),* edited by H.I. McCubbin, E.A. Thompson, A.I. Thompson, and J.E. Fromer, Boston: Sage (1995), pp. 143–158.

In human services, interventions are targeted toward causes or symptoms, and the relationships between interventions and symptoms are measured. The more we learn about a problem or person, the more we are able to isolate the factors that have contributed to those symptoms and prescribe a treatment. Through evaluation research, we try to measure whether interventions actually bring about observed outcomes. If we can demonstrate a cause-and-effect relationship between a helping intervention and the resolution of a problem, we can usually find the support to conduct the service.

The linear model's strength is that it is measurable. It promotes new knowledge and drives new ideas. It stretches what we know, because we are always seeking better interventions. But it tends to miss the whole person. The linear view is narrow. The more education we receive, the more we know about narrower and narrower fields of knowledge. Each discipline sees a different set of cause-and-effect relationships, and each believes, first and foremost, in its own view. The linear world view also believes that the problem resides in the person. It regards problems as largely individual. People and their symptoms become the objects of treatment, and success is measured by changes in individual symptoms.

THE RELATIONAL VIEW

The relational world view is rooted in tribal culture, and not just American Indian; it is the essence of many cultures' world views. It is intuitive, nontemporal, and fluid. Balance and harmony in relationships among multiple variables, including metaphysical forces, make up the core of the thought system. Every event is in relation to all other events, regardless of time, space, or physical existence. Health exists only when things are in harmony.

In the relational world view, service providers understand problems through the balances and imbalances in a person's relational world. Complex, sometimes illogical, interrelationships can be influenced by entering the client's context and manipulating the balance contextually, cognitively and emotionally, physically, and spiritually. Interventions need not be logically targeted to particular symptoms or causes, but rather focus on bringing the person back into balance. Nothing in a person's existence can change without all other things being changed as well. Thus, an effective helper gains understanding of the complex interdependent nature of life and learns how to use physical, psychological, contextual, and spiritual forces to promote harmony.

In the relational world view, four major forces must come into balance—context, mind, body, and spirit. Context includes culture, community, family, peers, work, school, and social history. The mind includes cognitive processes—thoughts, memories, and knowledge—and emotional processes, such as feelings, defenses, and self-esteem. The body comprises all physical aspects, such as genetics, gender, physical condition, sleep, nutrition, and substance use. The spiritual includes teachings and practices and metaphysical or innate forces.

These forces are in constant flux. You are not the same person at 4:00 p.m. that you were at 7:00 a.m. Your level of sleep is different, your nutrition is different, and your context is likely to be different. Thus, behavior is different, feelings are different, and what you think about is different. The system is constantly balancing itself as you change thoughts, feelings, physical state, or spiritual state. If you are able to stay in balance, you are said to be healthy. We have the capacity as humans to keep our own balance, for the most part, and our different cultures provide mechanisms to assist in this process—such as spiritual teachings, social skills and norms, dietary rules, and family roles.

Death, for example, is an event that threatens harmony. When we lose loved ones, we feel grief. Physically, we may cry, lose our appetite, or not sleep well. Spiritually, we have a learned positive response—rituals called funerals. Usually, they are community events, so the context is changed. We bring in relatives, friends, and supporters. In that context, we intellectualize about the dead person. We may recall and tell stories about her or him. We may intellectualize about death itself or be reminded of our cultural views of death. Physically, we touch others, hug, shake hands, eat, and shed tears.

These experiences are interdependent, playing off each other in interactions that, if successful, allow us to resolve grief by maintaining the balance. If we cannot, then, in Western culture, we are said to have unresolved grief, or, in some tribal cultures, to have a ghost sickness or to be bothered by a spirit. Different world views often use different conceptual language to describe the same phenomenon.

Natural Healers

Most social workers do not know why therapeutic relationships work, they just know they are helpful. From a relational world view, I know why they work: To form a relationship with somebody, one must become part of that person's context; by becoming part of the context, you change the balance. By entering the context in a way that supports, nurtures, or brings about positive changes through the balancing process, you will do some good. For some people, just having this context manipulation is enough to feel better, but others need more.

Natural healers of native cultures become part of the context and thereby have immediate impacts. Some natural helpers work intellectually. They give advice, tell stories, or give examples about how others have handled problems. Some natural healers intervene by offering riddles. By the time the person uncovers the answer, the problem is gone because the practitioner changed the way the person thinks about the problem.

When I use the terms natural helper or natural healer, people ask, "Do you mean a medicine man?" Not necessarily. Natural helpers and natural healers are all around us in our cultures. They are people to whom we turn for advice, help, support, and comfort. They may have specialized skills with spiritual or physical interventions. Some natural healers are just great listeners or nurturers—maybe grandparents, aunts, or uncles—who offer a chance for catharsis. There is nothing like a hug from a grandmother or a pat on the shoulder from an aunt to bolster you in difficult times.

Many Indian people work in the physical way. Some of our spiritual teachers treat mental health or relationship problems with herbs. Connecting an herbal remedy with a marital problem may seem unusual, but they are trying to manipulate the balance, not attack the issue in a linear way. Some practitioners use fasting, sweating, or other physical interventions to bring change.

There are many spiritual interventions. Some natural healers teach how to pray or how to do particular ceremonies. They may teach the belief system about death and dying, for example. Other practitioners perform healing rituals to block negative influences.

The sweat lodge is a traditional Native American intervention, frequently used in alcohol treatment, that approaches all systems simultaneously. One never enters the sweat lodge alone; there is always somebody there, thus setting the context. There is always teaching, thus providing an intellectual framework. People also frequently have emotional reactions. Those are the mental aspects. People experience vivid memories or visions—the spiritual. Finally, the body certainly changes through sweating for an hour, and the steam is cleansing. When you come out, you feel different: You have gone through a rebalancing. The sweat lodge does not make the person not drink, but rather helps the person restore balance and harmony.

FAMILY RESILIENCE

When I look for resilience within Indian families, I look for the holistic and complex interrelationships that allow families to survive and grow strong. Our strengths and challenges become evident if we examine family resilience from the relational perspective.

The Contextual

Indian families function in a context filled with strength-producing, harmonizing resources. Oppression, for all its damage, has created for all people of color an environment that develops and sharpens survival skills. We learn to recognize when we are welcome and when we are not. We teach our children to recognize subtle clues that may spell danger. We sit with our children in the movies or in front of the TV and interpret, cushioning the assaults of the mainstream media. We learn to cope with the dynamics of difference and pass on strategies to our children.

Our rich heritage provides an anchor that holds us to who we are. Our relatives often form interdependent systems of care. Healthy interdependence is the core of the extended family, neither fostering dependence nor stifling independence. Rather, everyone contributes in some way without expectation of reciprocity. I give my cousin a ride to the store, where she buys some items for our grandmother, who is home watching my brother's children, who are planning to wash my car when I return home. The support cycles throughout the family.

The community provides additional influences. From churches to social organizations to politics, we are affected by the events in the world around us. Family resilience is supported by role models, community norms, church structures, elders, and natural helpers.

The Mental

Sitting around the kitchen table or on the front steps, we learn strategies for interacting with the world. Passing on the stories of our lives, we pass skills to our children, parenting for resiliency. Storytelling is perhaps our greatest teaching resource for communicating identity, values, and lifeskills. The stories also tell us who our people are and what they stand for, providing role models and subtle expectations.

Emotionally, we learn many defenses that help us deal with overwhelming odds. Denial, splitting, disassociation, and projection are useful mechanisms for surviving oppression. Many of our families know real pain and endure grief almost beyond the comprehension of middle America, yet they give back to their communities. Because of oppression, substance abuse, or poverty, many have learned not to need, not to feel, and not to talk about it. Yet they still help at the church, at school, or within their families. These kindnesses bring the life-sustaining energy that flows from an aunt's approving looks, from a child's laughter, or from a pat on the back.

The Physical

The physical often concerns the body, but it also refers to family structure and roles. How we relate to our kin and sustain each other greatly influences the balance in our lives.

A 1993 study of Native American families found the roles of fathers to be central in either contributing to or preventing child neglect.[†] When fathers were involved in their families, child neglect was much less likely. Fathers did not have to be present in the home—only to remain contributing members of their families and to maintain relationships with their children. Families are more resilient if fathers contribute positively to the balance.

One thing families often do together is eat. Our special cultural or family foods, our use of foods to mark special occasions, and rituals around eating together are central contributions to the health of the family.

The Spiritual

Spiritual influences include both positive and negative practices. The positive are those we learn from spiritual disciplines or teachings: faith, prayer, meditation, healing ceremonies, even positive thinking. Negative practices are things like curses, the evil eye, or bad medicine. Even things like sin, promotion of chaos, and perpetuation of confusion are negative spiritual behaviors.

Folk teachings and spiritual institutions play great roles here. In tribal communities and other communities of color, the church or

---

† K. Nelson, M. Landsman, & T.L. Cross (1994). *Family Functioning of Neglectful Families: Final Report.* Iowa City: National Resource Center on Family Based Services.

traditional spiritual disciplines play significant roles in shaping families' spiritual practices. The beliefs and customs that go with them provide much of the energy needed to face adversity.

Human behavior is also influenced by spiritual forces beyond our making. Luck, grace, karma, helping spirits, and angelic intervention are terms that describe getting the right help at the right time. One does not have to practice a spiritual discipline to experience the phenomena. Bad luck, bad karma, ghosts, the devil, and misfortune describe the things that bother people no matter what their spiritual practices. These forces are often controlled through prayer, ritual, or ceremony. Some see these influences as driven by external metaphysical forces; others see them driven purely by chance. Whatever the belief system, these natural forces are always in play and thus challenge and strengthen the family.

All Together

So what contributes to family resilience? It is not the extended family, spirituality, or the role of fathers. It is the complex interplay among all these things. It is the harmony we can achieve when they come together. We promote resilience by contributing to the balance.

Western helping methods split the person. We give physicians the body, educators and psychologists the mind, social workers the context, and clergy the spirit. Each looks at the same person and finds different definitions of the problems and different solutions. Physicians medicate them away, educators teach them away, psychologists counsel them away, social workers advocate them away, and clergy pray them away—and each is unable to communicate effectively to the other what the problems are or what to do about them.

The relational model has its weaknesses. It seeks harmony at the expense of individuals. For example, a family will try to compensate by taking care of an alcoholic, often by helping the alcoholic drink. Codependent behaviors prevail until the person becomes so sick that the system can no longer stay in harmony and breaks apart. This weakness becomes a strength, however, once recovery begins in the family system or community.

The linear model dominates family services, yet almost half of clients nationwide hold a relational world view. Helpers and families come to the helping relationship with different world views, different concepts of the problems, and different potential solutions. As long as the mainstream is unable to acknowledge the relational model as valid, cultural competence remains elusive. Families of color will continue to be resilient, but in spite of the helping system rather than because of it.